Entering the Healing Ground

ENTERING THE HEALING GROUND

The Wild Edge of Sorrow
OFFICIAL WORKBOOK

FRANCIS WELLER
WITH BEVIN DONAHUE

North Atlantic Books
Huichin, unceded Ohlone land
Berkeley, California

North Atlantic Books
Huichin, unceded Ohlone land
2526 Martin Luther King Jr. Way
Berkeley, CA 94704 USA
www.northatlanticbooks.com

Cover art © basel101658 via Shutterstock
Cover design by Jasmine Hromjak
Book design by Happenstance Type-O-Rama

Printed in Canada

Entering the Healing Ground: The Wild Edge of Sorrow Official Workbook is sponsored and published by North Atlantic Books, an educational nonprofit that collaborates with partners to develop cross-cultural perspectives; nurture holistic views of art, science, the humanities, and healing; and seed personal and global transformation by publishing work on the relationship of body, spirit, and nature.

North Atlantic Books's publications are distributed to the US trade and internationally by Penguin Random House Publisher Services. For further information, visit our website at www.northatlanticbooks.com.

The authorized representative in the EU for product safety and compliance is Eucomply OÜ, Pärnu mnt 139b-14, 11317 Tallinn, Estonia, hello@eucompliancepartner.com, +33757690241.

ISBN: 979-8-88984-331-3 (paperback) ISBN: 979-8-88984-332-0 (ebook)

1 2 3 4 5 6 7 8 9 FRIESENS 30 29 28 27 26

This book includes recycled material and material from well-managed forests.

To the growing circle of grief tenders

Contents

Acknowledgments

First and foremost, I wish to thank Bevin Donahue of North Atlantic Books for her excellent skills at crafting this workbook. She was clearly attuned to the soul of *The Wild Edge of Sorrow*, and it shows in the subtle and palpable ways that this book invites the reader deeper into the material.

To North Atlantic Books for our ongoing collaborations. I have felt well-tended by everyone there and look forward to future creations together.

To the many grief ritual participants over the last twenty-five years for bringing your courage, vulnerability, and your own wild edges to our gatherings. You taught me much about how to be with sorrow and loss in a sacred manner.

To the poets, teachers, and tenders of the wild imagination who have kept the thread of soul alive in this difficult time. You continue to remind us of the need to tend the river of images that arise from within and without. This is how we keep the world alive. All praise!

To the green world and her exuberant display of beauty and power, especially all my kin in the Russian River Watershed. You have fed my soul for many decades and continue to be a source of solace and renewal: The towhees and blue jays, oaks and maples, foxes and fawns, redwoods and huckleberries, and so many others. I am grateful to be nested in this rich web of relations. Remaining connected to this wider network of kinship keeps me close to this breathing, animate world.

I am profoundly grateful for my soul lineage, that astonishing reservoir of wisdom and remembrance that winds its way down the arc of time. Thank you for the amazing inheritance that nurtures me daily.

And I acknowledge you, dear reader, for your willingness to help pick up the ragged threads in our communal coat of belonging. Your tears help us wash off the dust of amnesia and recall our place within the folds of this aching and beautiful world. Bless you.

Preface

Dear Reader,

Welcome and thank you for choosing this official workbook for *The Wild Edge of Sorrow*. This workbook, carefully crafted with devotion and a beautiful attention to the soul of the material, is a place to explore and engage the weighty cargo of grief in your life. One of the central requirements of our time is developing the capacity to metabolize the many tributaries of sorrow that will touch our lives in the coming years.

You may have found your way to this workbook because you feel the growing web of loss touching every element of your life. Or maybe you are here because you sense the increasing reality of the *Long Dark*, perhaps without even knowing how to name this time and feeling. I imagine, like so many others, you sense something is moving out there, in the collective field, and it can cast an anxious shiver over all our daily lives.

You may be here out of love for this beautiful, aching world. You long to offer something to ease her suffering. You may be experiencing a sense of overwhelm or a degree of bewilderment about how to respond to these tenuous times. These feelings are understandable, arising, in part, from a sense of isolation and the long legacy of individualism that have conditioned us to feel as if we must face these waves of grief alone. *This is not true. We are not alone.*

A central intention for this workbook is to offer a felt sense of being part of a wider circle of grief tenders. As you respond to the questions, ritual invitations, and meditations, know that you are joining many others undertaking a similar pilgrimage into the heart of sorrow. Knowing we are part of a network of connections responding to the cumulative losses surrounding us is fortifying. It offers encouragement, strength, and a sense of ballast. *We cannot possibly respond to the immense currents of grief alone.* Realizing we are part of an emergent community of soul activists helps us maintain our affection for this tender, struggling world.

We have entered a prolonged season of descent, taking us down into a territory familiar to soul—grief, vulnerability, loss, and uncertainty, bending toward mystery. In the language of ancient Greece, we are in a time of *katabasis*, when we are taken downward into the underworld. We are being asked to descend and undertake the work in this shadowed terrain. Learning to keep our grief moving is part of the core curriculum for the Long Dark. Staying current with our sorrow enables us to remain present to the currents of soul and the *anima mundi*.

The ambient field in which we live is saturated with sorrow, anxiety, despair, and an uneasy sense that the world we once knew and relied upon is rapidly fading. Much of what we encounter these days is not personal, not rooted in our histories or intrapsychic matters. We are actively inundated by losses occurring in the wider collective, culturally and environmentally. This can feel overwhelming and can easily overshadow our personal losses and heartbreaks. Every loss is worthy of our care and attention, from the most intimate to the collective. Every loss is significant to the heart and soul. We must honor all the losses that come into our lives.

Throughout *The Wild Edge of Sorrow*, I reference the need to take up *an apprenticeship with sorrow*. Our apprenticeship is a form of ripening and maturation, a long discipline, a devotional practice to become skilled in the craft and art of loss. Our apprenticeship is rooted in building soul muscle, stamina for the coming season, as well as patience and a robust spaciousness capable of welcoming whatever arrives at our door. Through our apprenticeship, we learn to hold complexity and uncertainty and to resist the cultural pull of amnesia and anesthesia. Grief work is an insurgent art, a powerful affirmation of life.

There are three premises at the heart of our apprenticeship. These premises point to a fundamental psychic necessity: We must transfer our sorrows into our adult hands. The first premise is that *grief is not only an emotion, but a core human faculty*. To be skillful in this terrain is to possess the capacity to turn toward the sorrows we encounter, and gradually transmute them into a medicine for the community. Pure alchemy!

It takes tremendous psychic strength to engage the materials of loss, the difficult emotions, the painful memories, the heavy cargo of sorrow. Our skills will be tempered over time through many encounters with loss. The apprenticeship is long.

The second premise is that *grief works us in profound ways, reshaping us day by day, like water on sandstone. And we are asked to work grief.* In other words, this is not a passive process. We come to see that the intention of this work is not simply endurance, hoping to get to the other side of the grief quickly, but also depth. We want to be deepened by our time with sorrow, carved and reshaped by the river of loss that eddies in and out of our lives.

The third premise is that *our apprenticeship is a sustained practice in the art of vesseling*. We are invited to learn how to hold, contain, separate, and warm the materials. This is an old alchemical thought: We must keep the material in the vessel warm to keep it moving and changing. This is done through attention, affection, interest, outrage, and efforts like writing, dancing, drawing, ritual, painting, and intimate conversations with trusted circles of people.

As you go through this workbook, these three premises will be brought into your direct engagement. You will build core skills at meeting sorrow, metabolizing it over time, gradually coming to see grieving as a central faculty of a mature human being. As you respond to the various questions and prompts, you will be working grief and not simply trying to get through it. And lastly, every time you return to the work nestled in these pages, you will be vesseling the material. Attention is vesseling.

This space is an invitation, an opportunity to work the ground of grief slowly, with patience, and in a manner that is not based on accomplishments but rather one rooted in self-compassion and soul.

It is essential that we undertake our psychological work, thereby deepening our inner capacities to help keep our small boat of self afloat and capable of responding meaningfully to the demands of the times. We are being initiated into the Clan of the Brokenhearted. Let us strengthen ourselves into the Clan of the Mended Hearted as we reach for the far shore of the Long Dark. Do the work. Stay connected. Love this world.

Blessings,
Francis Weller
Russian River Watershed

Introduction
Entering the Healing Ground

*"To honor our grief, to grant it space and time in our frantic world, is to fulfill a covenant with soul—to welcome all that is, thereby granting room for our most authentic life."** *

"Grief and loss touch us all."

When we gather in community for a grief ritual—when we hold each other's sadnesses, pains, shames, and regrets together—we come to acknowledge that our sorrows are shared. Both grief and healing are communal endeavors. This workbook is designed to hold space for an inclusive conversation between our singular experiences and the soul of the world—to come into relationship with our losses, to see that "our broken hearts have the potential to open us to a wider sense of identity."

This workbook will guide you through *The Wild Edge of Sorrow: Rituals of Renewal and the Sacred Work of Grief.* You can complete it chapter by chapter, dip in and out, or return to it after reading the book in full. Your journey here doesn't need to be linear.

When you're ready, find a quiet, comfortable place to begin.

Preface and Introduction: Questions for Reflection

1. Our world has many sources of loss: the death of a loved one; ecological devastation; the end of a relationship; futures disrupted by war and

---

* All of Francis Weller's quotations in this workbook are from *The Wild Edge of Sorrow: Rituals of Renewal and the Sacred Work of Grief* (North Atlantic Books, 2025).

genocide; and many more. Most of us are grieving more than one loss at the same time. This constellation of sorrow can be immense.

What brings you to this book today? If you're not quite sure yet, that's okay too.

2. Francis Weller writes, "Grief and love are sisters, woven together from the beginning. Their kinship reminds us that there is no love that does not contain loss and no loss that is not a reminder of the love we carry for what we once held close."

Reflect on this quote. What do you think about the relationship between grief and love?

Think of this quote in relationship to your own life and your own losses. What comes to the fore? Have you experienced a connection between the depth of your grief and the size of your love?

"It takes outrageous courage to face outrageous loss."

3. Grief isn't always personal: Sometimes it occurs on an immense or global scale. When grief from habitat destruction, climate crisis, or community catastrophe stops us in our tracks, we face what Weller calls a "crack in our denial." What do you think he means?

Have you experienced a "crack in your denial"? What did it feel like? How would you visualize it?

4. As a culture, why do you think we build up armor against grief and loss?

When you're in a safe and comfortable place to do so, take a quiet moment. Think about a loss that you feel deeply, but that isn't personal to you. This could be anything from climate disaster to systemic injustice to conflict or violence.

What emotions are you feeling? Below are some example phrases to inspire your reflection:

- "I feel sad."
- "I feel helpless."
- "I am angry."

Focus on one emotion. What does it feel like in your body?

How do you think this feeling connects to your grief?

What might it feel like to honor these feelings? It's okay if you don't know. Below are examples of some of the ways a person might approach and engage newly uncovered emotions:

- "I want to do something about it."
- "I acknowledge I need help."
- "I will sit with these feelings."
- "I will let myself feel these feelings."
- "I will process these feelings."

5. "Learning to welcome, hold, and metabolize these sorrows is the work of a lifetime."

What do you think Weller means by this?

What do you think it means to have a "relationship with loss"?

Do you have a relationship with grief?

If you do, what is it like? It's okay if you don't, or if you're not sure.

Has your relationship with loss and grief changed or evolved over time? If so, how?

If you're unsure, or if you haven't thought much about your relationship with loss and grief, that's okay. Think about why you might want to do this work. How could building a relationship with grief help you or teach you something new? You can also come back to this question later.

> *"Bringing grief and death out of the shadow is our spiritual responsibility, our sacred duty. By so doing, we may be able to feel our desire for life once again and remember who we are, where we belong, and what is sacred."*

6. Weller notes that we live in a "grief-phobic and death-denying society." What do you think he means?

Do you see this show up in your day-to-day life, in your family, or in your community? How so?

What do you think could be different about your own life and relationships if you welcomed grief out of the shadows?

What do you think could be different about the world or your community if we each did this work? If we did this work together?

7. Weller says, "Grief is always, in some way, accompanying us." It's a universal experience, yet many of us carry grief alone. Why do you think this is?

8. Have you ever had to carry grief on your own? If so, what was it like? What does it feel like to reflect back on it now?

9. Have you ever grieved together in community? If so, what was it like? Did you find anything unexpected, sacred, or meaningful in these connected communal experiences? Did it make your grief feel heavier, lighter, harder, softer, or none of those things?

Practice
The Generous Heart—The Gift of Self-Compassion*

This practice invites you to move toward non-judgment and self-compassion as you get to know, and then deepen, your relationship with grief.

Entering a conversation with grief is a sacred endeavor. It asks a lot of us. Many different—and sometimes unexpected—emotions, memories, thoughts, or sensations can rise to the surface.

Coming to be with yourself from a place of what Weller calls "non-self-improvement" helps us shed some of our culture's obsession with perfection. If we can engage in this work without attachment to an outcome (or a fixation on "being the best"), we can allow ourselves simply to *be*. This means that we can access a deeper "capacity to welcome what is, what comes, [and] whoever arrives at the interior door of our soul's house."

This is essential grounding for the work to come.

---

* "The Generous Heart: The Gift of Self-Compassion" practice is rooted in Buddhist teachings and appears in the resources section at the end of *The Wild Edge of Sorrow*.

THE PRACTICE

"One of the working definitions that I hold is that self-compassion is the *internalized village*. Pause for a moment and think about how we tend to respond to a friend who is suffering. Usually, we feel an immediate caring and sympathy in our heart toward their pain. We don't typically recoil in judgment or condemnation, and yet, that is often how we respond to our own moments of pain. Imagine, instead, that these dear people in our lives are dwelling inside us, that the little village in our world has been taken into our hearts. Now, when suffering arises, our interior friend can say to us, 'Be gentle. Be kind. Be compassionate with this suffering part of your life.' It is soothing to imagine the village residing inside our chest. Perhaps the Golden Rule needs an addendum: 'Do unto yourself as you would do unto others.' This *pilgrimage of friendship* toward our own life is essential."

Return to this invitation to self-compassion as often as you need to as you read *The Wild Edge of Sorrow*, and as you move more deeply into your own work with grief and loss.

An Invitation to Ritual Creating a Grief Shrine

As you begin this exploration, you are encouraged to create a space in your home to hold vigil for all that arises as you engage the material in this workbook. Much will be stirred as you respond to the invitations in the book. Setting up a space to notice and attend to this rich ore is an extension of self-compassion as you learn to tend the various sources of sorrow in your life with warmth and care.

A shrine is a place of attention and focus, of remembrance and reverence. It is a place of return and connection, a form of vesseling allowing the tender pieces of loss and sorrow to be kept close to our awareness. A shrine is a container necessary to cook what is in the vessel.

As you build your shrine, hold in your thoughts, "What kind of space would be most welcoming of my grief?" It could be very simple: a candle and a flower. You may want to bring some beauty into the space: colored cloths, stones, greens, sacred objects. You could also adorn your shrine with images of ancestors, personal and communal, and images of those who have left the world that have touched your heart and soul: species, qualities, cultures.

You may also want to place an object or two on the shrine that speaks to the obstacles you encounter on your way to honoring your losses. Fear, shame, and isolation are all worth including on the shrine and, in fact, are often sources of grief themselves.

Tend your shrine. Keep the flowers fresh, the water clear. Return to this space regularly. Repetition is an essential part of soul maintenance. The work is to keep your grief warm. Spending time at the shrine is a way to extend your affection to what it is you are grieving. While you do so, know that there are many others tending their shrines along with you. You are part of a multicentric shrine.

Chapter 1

AN APPRENTICESHIP
WITH SORROW

*"We are remade in times of grief, broken apart
and reassembled. It is hard, painful, and unbidden work.
No one goes in search of loss; rather, it finds us and
reminds us of the temporary gift we have been
given, these few sweet breaths we call life."*

Chapter 1: Questions for Reflection

1. Weller says, "It was through the dark waters of grief that I came to touch
    my unlived life, by at last unleashing tears I had never shed for the losses
    in my world. Grief led me back into a world that was vivid and radiant.
    There is some strange intimacy between grief and aliveness, some sacred
    exchange between what seems unbearable and what is most exquisitely
    alive. Through this, I have come to have a lasting faith in grief."

    Does Weller's experience of the relationship between *grief* and *aliveness*
    ring true to you? Why or why not?

2. Weller says, "This book is also about restoring the *soul of the world*." What
    do you think he means by this?

    What does the "soul of the world" mean to you?

3. How do you tune into the rhythms of nature in your regular, day-to-day
    life? This can be anything from listening to birdsong to tending a plant,

from spending time with an animal friend to being outside, if you have access to green space.

Pause for a moment and reflect: What parts of nature do you feel most connected to?

Is there a particular element or landscape that you feel drawn to in moments of sadness, suffering, or grief?

As you hold this connection, what sights, smells, feelings, sounds, and sensations come up for you?

4. Weller describes his experience of profound grief after a catastrophic oil spill in the Gulf of Mexico. Have you ever experienced grief in response to environmental disasters, habitat destruction, or wildlife loss?

What did it feel like?

Did you share how you were feeling with anyone else? Why or why not?

If you had a response—like anger or numbness—that wasn't legible to you as grief, that's okay. What other feelings or sensations were you aware of in the moment? What do you feel now when you think back to this experience?

Are there any other emotions sitting underneath responses like anger, numbness, or shock? If so, what do you think those feelings might be trying to communicate?

"Grief and loss are with us continually, shaping our walk through life, and in some real way, determining how fully we engage our lives."

"When we come to our grief with reverence, we find ourselves in right relationship with sorrow, neither too far away nor too close."

5. Weller writes, "For us to tolerate the rigors of engaging the images, emotions, memories, and dreams that arise in times of grief, we need to fortify

our interior ground." He also writes, "Grief work is not passive: it implies an ongoing practice of deepening, attending, and listening."

What do you think it means to "fortify your interior ground"?

Why do you think this is necessary? How might it prepare you for the active state of grief work?

6. In order to function in daily life, many of us need to put on filters. If we respond to and truly hold every sorrow, loss, and grief we encounter, we would likely fall into paralysis or despair. Creating distance can help us move through the world, but it can also anesthetize us, or close us off from connection and intimacy. Weller notes, "What had been severed for the sake of our preservation must now be rejoined for the sake of our healing."

What do you think he means?

Are there any sorrows hovering at your periphery that haven't been fully held or metabolized? This could look like many things: a beloved natural space being cleared for development; a lingering sadness for an experience you didn't get to have; loss related to an illness that you haven't truly explored; and more.

Why do you think you haven't processed this pain or loss? Some examples might be:

- "I don't have the time."
- "I'm afraid of falling apart."
- "I feel helpless to change it, so I try to ignore it."
- "I don't have the time to process it."
- "I'm too focused on being there for other people."
- "I need to focus on material needs like making ends meet."

7. Weller writes, "Every mature culture has guided its people in this apprenticeship with grief. Underlying this education is an acknowledgment of our spiritual indebtedness to the cosmos for all we are given to sustain us day to day. These cultures honor this truth and have based their ritual life and teachings around it."

What is your culture's relationship with grief? What kinds of rituals exist to honor grief and loss?

If you're having trouble coming up with a response, that's okay. That's an answer, too—in what ways is your culture *not* in relationship with grief? Why do you think that might be?

What do you wish were different?

8. "Grief is alive, wild, untamed; it cannot be domesticated." Is this your experience of grief? In what ways (or not)?

Practice Deepening Your Kinship with the Living Earth

We are each a part of nature: The rhythms, actions, and arcs of our lives are interwoven with the living earth. This remains true even when the pace and demands of modern-day life conspire to make us forget.

Rediscovering our connection to the natural world can facilitate profound experiences of wonder, awe, wisdom, and joy. It can also guide us back into balance, reminding us to be better carers and stewards. Some of the prompts above invited you to reflect on your existing relationship to nature, and to begin holding these connections with curiosity and intention.

Your relationship with the earth can be a source of support in times of grief, loss, and pain. It can also be a source of connection, gratitude, and beauty in any season of your life. You should tend to this relationship with regular care—to nurture and give back to it, too. This practice helps you think about, and deepen, this relationship. This exercise is individualized and designed to be open-ended; each of your answers will be unique to you. The end goal is to discover ways of connecting that are personally meaningful. Your practice—and what you get from it—may change and evolve in the ways that all relationships, over time, do.

When you have some time, return to this earlier question: What parts of nature do you feel most connected to? Asked another way: What part of nature feels most sacred to you? Is it a singular place? An element? An animal, plant, habitat, or ecosystem? What aspects of it make you feel connected to the greater web of life, as if you yourself are part of something larger and ancient? Has this feeling or connection always existed, or is it new? Can you remember the first time you felt it? If not, imagine what it may have felt like to discover it: Did you experience wonder? Awe? Fear? Calm? Something else?

Meditate on how you interact with this sacredness. Do you observe, sit next to, or move with it? Do you touch, hear, smell, or taste it? Is this experience time-bound, related to a seasonal migration or change, or accessible all year round? Is it right outside your door, or do you have to put in some effort to get to it? Do you practice this relationship during the day, at night, or does the timing change? Are there any specific actions or habits that you notice you already do? Are there any actions that would feel natural, meaningful, or ineffably "right" to take as you engage with these parts of nature that feel most sacred to you?

Consider what actions feel meaningful. What do you want your new or renewed relationship with the living earth to look, feel, and be like? When do you feel most connected or at peace? Is it when you're silent, still, and observing? Or active, engaging, and creating? What do you imagine your chosen sacredness may want to hear from you? What actions—offerings, words, movements, creations— feel appropriate? What would enrich your knowing and sense of connection with this sacredness?

Set your container. This work derives much of its power from the places, spaces, times, practices, and other parameters that signal: *You've entered ritual time; this is holy ground.* Ritual practice exists outside the definitions of our "normal" lives. It adheres to special rules, and asks us to exist in more mindful, intentional, and reverent ways. Think through: What do I want my container of practice to be like? How might time of day, ritual setting, or music lend greater meaning to this work? What objects, words, or offerings might honor my connection to the natural world? How do I open my practice? How do I close it?

Experiment with ritual. See what works. Be open to feedback from your inner self and your surroundings. Reconsider and reshape what doesn't feel quite right yet, or anything that feels misaligned with the intentions and meaning you bring to this work. Come to it with an attitude of reverence and curiosity. Revisit your frequency, your offerings, and how you open and close the ritual space. As you interact with and deepen your kinship with the living world, remember that it's not only your ritual practices—but the relationship itself—that will be there to offer you support and steady grounding as you move through times of grief, uncertainty, and heartbreak.

Meditation Practice The Fortified Ground

When you can find a moment away from distractions and obligations, come to a safe, quiet, and comfortable place.

Imagine yourself at your most "fortified"—what does this look like for you? Are you resourced? Open? Peaceful? What other words, ideas, or feelings would you choose to embody as you fortify yourself to enter the healing ground?

Now, take a moment to imagine what this could feel like in your body. Would you be relaxed? Alert? What would your posture be like? What might be different about how you breathe and move? What might be the same?

Breathe into and embody this sense of fortification. What would it be like to bring it into your "regular" day?

An Invitation for Deeper Reflection
Opening the Conversation

Grief work is soul work. To engage with our grief—to really feel it, get to know it, and hear its profound teachings—requires us to be in active conversation with it. We must invite it in and allow it to change us. Grief works us as we work grief. This work is a two-way street: The more we dialogue, explore, and come to our grief with openness and humility, the more we'll receive its wisdom . . . and be transformed in new and often unexpected ways.

Entering into a conversation with grief isn't easy, especially in a culture that embodies denial, repression, and forward momentum at any cost. Allowing the time and emotional space to accept grief, loss, and all the feelings and sensations that accompany them can be a tall order. This reality has warped our relationship to grief. In some cases, it's severed our ability to feel deeply into many, or even most, of our emotions.

When you have some time and access to a quiet place, read and reflect on the following quote:

> "How do we learn to carry our grief and not collapse or turn away in denial? How do we come to see grief as vital and necessary and not something only to be endured? To achieve this shift requires a re-visioning of grief, not as an event in our lives—*a period of mourning*—but as an ongoing conversation that accompanies us throughout life."

Close your eyes and visualize grief. This can be a particular experience of your own grief, or the idea of capital-G Grief. Hold this image or feeling in your mind.

Observe what comes up for you in response. Do you feel uncomfortable? Fearful? Tired? Angry? Reactive? Do you feel like it's here to cause hurt or harm? Does it hang around the edges of your periphery, or does it try to engage with you? Is it present all the time, or does it make itself known in singular moments of pain and loss?

As you reflect on what comes up, gently invite yourself to *re-vision your grief*. What would your concept of grief look and feel like if it were here as a teacher, guide, or companion? How might its essence be transformed in your mind? Are there any imagined traits—like its weight or felt presence—that would shift?

Try imagining this. Then imagine inviting this re-visioned grief to your table. What questions would you ask it? What questions would it ask of you? How would the conversation go? Think about other times that you entered into relationships that may have felt scary or uncomfortable at first, but evolved into wise, necessary, or enriching experiences. What changed? How did you open yourself up, and why did you stay the course? Think about this in relationship to grief. Try to hold this with openness and, as it feels right, invite it to accompany you on your journey through this workbook.

Chapter 2

TO AND FROM THE SOUL'S HALL

"There are few things as genuine as a person grieving.
There are no questions to ask, no wondering what someone
is feeling. It is self-evident. We are revealing the heartache
we carry, the sorrows we have shouldered for decades.
We are in the tumult of releasing our tears. This is
a holy night, and we go on for hours."

Chapter 2: Questions for Reflection

1. Weller writes the above when describing the communal sharing of grief. Have you ever processed your grief with others? If yes, what was it like? If not, what do you think it might be like?

2. "We need to create circles of welcome in our lives in order to keep leaning into the world; to keep moving grief through our psyches and bodies, so we can taste the sweetness of life," Weller writes.

   Who is in your "circle of welcome"? Do you have a community to hold you in times of loss or pain?

   What would your ideal "village" look like?

   How do you want to be witnessed and held in community in times of grief?

   What unique gifts or perspectives can you offer to support others as they move through loss?

3. "Belonging protects the heart from much of life's unavoidable challenges." What does "belonging" mean to you?

> *"It is our unexpressed sorrows, the congested stories of loss, that, when left unattended, block our access to the soul. To be able to freely move in and out of the soul's inner chapters, we must first clear the way."*

4. "The territory of grief is heavy." When you have a quiet moment and it feels comfortable to do so, close your eyes. Think about the word *grief*. Turn it over in your mind—what does it feel like? What shape does it hold? Does Weller's description of grief as "heavy" feel true to you?

   What other images, feelings, sensations, and descriptions come up for you? Feel free to draw them, write them down, sing or dance them out, or express them in whatever way feels right to you. Try not to hold back.

   What was it like to experience your relationship to the word *grief* in this way?

5. Weller describes both the felt senses and practical impacts of grief: "At times, grief invites us into a terrain that reduces us to our most naked self. We find it hard to meet the day, to accomplish the smallest of tasks, to tolerate the greetings of others. We feel estranged from the world and only marginally able to navigate the necessities of eating, sleeping, and self-care. Some other presence takes over in times of intense grief, and we are humbled, brought to our knees. We live close to the ground, the gravity of sorrow felt deep in our bones."

   What is the experience of grief like for you? How does it change your day-to-day tasks, habits, and abilities? Does it show up in your interactions with others or shape your behaviors? Explore below. Try to avoid placing judgment on any of your answers or experiences, simply noting what is or has been.

6. In this chapter, Weller describes a few cultural practices that make space for grief. One is a "time out of time" that encourages the bereaved to descend into the depths of their grief and get to know it.

What do you think it means to have a "time out of time"? Have you ever experienced this kind of state?

Does your community or culture have a practice like this? What about your ancestral culture(s)? Describe below any practices you know about or any you discover from research.

What elements speak to you? Which elements might not? If you're moved to do so, try putting your thoughts on paper in writing or drawing.

*"We must honor the needs of
the soul during times of grief."*

7. "Grief both acknowledges what has been lost and ensures that we don't forget what must be remembered." Weller refers to "non-redemptive mourning" here. What do you think it means to experience pain and loss without focusing on redemption?

8. "Some grief is not meant to be resolved and set aside. Sometimes grief helps us hold what must be carried by a people so that they never have to endure such pain again," Weller writes.

    What kinds of losses do you think we need to keep present in our communal memory? Why?

    How might being present to our grief keep these kinds of losses from occurring again?

9. Can you think of examples where unmetabolized grief has resulted in cycles of harm? What are they?

    What impact does this have on an individual level? On a community or cultural level?

10. Reflect on this quote: "There is a direct relationship between mourning and memory. To counter the amnesia of our times, we must be willing to look into the face of the loss and keep it nearby. In this way, we may be able to honor the losses and live our lives as carriers of their unfinished stories. This is an ancient thought—how we tend the dead is as important as how we tend the living."

    What comes up for you in response to this passage?

Exercise: Carrying Unfinished Stories

Western culture places great importance on progress: We're supposed to move on, move up, and keep going in all aspects of our lives . . . no matter what else is going on around (or within) us. But as Weller notes, this isn't how humans are made. How does a fixation with progress disconnect us from more natural rhythms of being?

What might this have to do with grief?

Consider: How would you choose to spend your time if you didn't have to labor, produce, or complete a lot of tasks? What activities, relationships, or experiences are most aligned with your soul?

What, for you, feels like a more "natural" way to stay in relationship with your grief than quickly "moving on" from the pain of loss?

What does it mean to have an "unfinished story"? When you can come to a quiet, peaceful place, meditate on the following question: What would it mean, to you, to live into the unfinished stories of your losses?

If you're moved to do so, try putting your thoughts on paper. Keep writing, letting your words come without judging, curating, or constraining them. What does it feel like to write into an "unfinished story"?

An Invitation to Ritual Talking Circles*

"The most basic ritual humans have been sharing for thousands of years is the talking circle. In this simple practice, everyone is invited to take some time to become present. This may be done through a guided meditation, meaningful poems or writings, or simply a period of silence. Following this, the circle is opened for people to share whatever grief they are carrying. It is important, however, to establish some basic agreements beforehand.

No advice should be given. Practice simply saying 'we hear you' or 'thank you' after someone shares.

Resist the temptation to provide answers. Remember, grief is not a problem to be solved, but an experience that needs to be witnessed.

Deep listening to what someone is sharing. Allow some breath and space after someone speaks. This fosters a feeling of being heard and the felt sense of the rich soil we are building together.

---

* The "Talking Circles" ritual appears in the resources section at the end of *The Wild Edge of Sorrow*.

Confidentiality. The experience of vulnerability and risk is a reflection of how safe the participants feel to be seen. It is important to agree that what is shared in the circle will be held within the circle.

Practice revelatory speech. This is speech that reveals who we are, not how someone else should be. Creating a safe container for mutual revelation is a healing process. It is simple ritual, yet few of us have been granted this type of sacred ground."

Chapter 3

THE FIVE GATES OF GRIEF

Over the course of our lives, grief enters our hearts in many ways. To acknowledge and tend to our grief, we must understand the thresholds that Weller names as the *Five Gates of Grief.*

Most of us are familiar with the first gate of grief, which is the sorrow we experience with the loss of someone or something we love. But the other gates receive little or no attention—and thus little or no care—in modern Western society.

The grief that accumulates at these thresholds remains untouched. And while we feel the weight of these unattended sorrows in our souls, we may not see them for what they are; we may have lost the ability to listen to what they're trying to say. We may not recognize that they are profound sites of wounding.

Chapter 3: Questions for Reflection

THE FIRST GATE: EVERYTHING WE LOVE, WE WILL LOSE

1. Weller shares a poem as well as his own thoughts on the innate relationship between love and loss. He says, "Grief is akin to praise" and "To love is to accept the rites of grief." How would you put this idea—that love and loss are inextricably woven together—into your own words?

2. If you're coming to this work because you've lost a loved one, what are your fears? What are your hopes? What does your soul tell you it needs on this journey of grief?

It's okay if you don't know, or if you're feeling some resistance coming up. You can use your own journal or the lined pages at the back of this workbook to ask more questions or write whatever feels true for you.

3. How do you think that grief honors your love? What could it look like to express your sorrow in a way that embodies this love? It's okay if other feelings come up here too.

4. The death of a beloved is an immense and unfathomable loss. What other kinds of sorrows meet us at the threshold of the first gate?

5. Why do you think Weller chose to include illness and suicide at this gate?

6. Do you think that our society offers a safe harbor to grieve non-death losses, like illness, loss of function, or physical deterioration? Do you think it's different for different people? Do you feel as if you're "allowed" to grieve these things for yourself or for others? Why or why not?

7. Have you ever experienced grief from an illness? Have you ever mourned the effects of illness in someone you love?

   If so, what was it like? Did you experience your feelings at the time as expressions of grief? Or did grief show up as other emotions?

8. The pain related to loss by suicide can be complex. This pain is often encountered differently than other kinds of death by society, our communities, and even our own families. Why do you think this is? What does this bring up for you, if anything? Any feeling is okay. If you can, try to notice what comes to the fore without judgment.

9. If you're mourning the loss of a loved one who died by suicide, what do you need as you come to this work? What might feel unique to your experience? What might require special care as you relate to this loss and your loved one's memory?

10. For readers mourning any kind of loss at the first gate, what support do you need from other people to support your grief journey?

   What permissions, spaciousness, or other considerations do you feel like you need from *yourself* to be open and present to the totality of your experience?

THE SECOND GATE: THE PLACES THAT HAVE NOT KNOWN LOVE

At the second threshold, we meet the grief that lives in the places of ourselves that haven't been touched by love.

1. Each of us is inherently worthy of love and care. Shame, society, past experiences, or lies that we may have been told about who we are can lead us to believe that we are undeserving. Are there parts of you that feel unloved?

2. Weller notes, "These neglected pieces of soul live in utter despair. What we perceive as defective about ourselves, we also experience as loss."

   Think about the parts of your own soul that feel neglected. Have you ever consciously recognized this neglect as a loss? Why or why not?

3. Many of us meet more than one loss at this threshold. If this is the case for you, focus on one that needs tending. Discern if you feel resourced enough to be in conversation with this sorrow. When you're ready, acknowledge the others and, for now, gently set them aside.

   What experience, belief, feeling, relationship, or part of your history did you choose to tend?

   How have you related to this in the past? How does it show up in your body? What about in your relationships or interactions with others? If you are having trouble getting started, here are some examples of insights that could come up:

   - "I pushed parts of my soul down."
   - "Neglecting my soul makes me feel angry."
   - "I take out that loss on other people."
   - "I withdraw from other people."
   - "I go numb."

4. When you're ready, seek out a quiet and comfortable space. If it feels okay to do so, close your eyes and begin to touch the edges of this sorrow. What does it feel like? What does it feel like in your body in this moment? It's okay to pause or take a break whenever you need.

5. Reflect on this quote from Weller: "The proper response to any loss is grief, but *we cannot grieve for something that we feel is outside the circle of worth.* That is our predicament—we chronically sense the presence of sorrow, but

we are unable to truly grieve, because we feel in our body that this piece of who we are is unworthy of grief."

As you reflect on the second gate, does this passage resonate with you? Are there pieces of your experience that you neglect because you don't know if they're worthy of care—or deserving of grief?

6. What would it mean to accept this part of yourself? What might be different if you did? Note anything that comes up. This could be fear, hope, relief, joy, or any other feeling that's true to you.

7. What do you need to grieve this loss? What support might you want from loved ones? Nature? Your community? How could you ask for what you need from others? What care can you grant to *yourself*?

8. What do you think will be healed or released when you grieve this loss?

9. What do you think Weller means by the term *premature death* in this section?

    What resonates with you about this idea? What doesn't?

10. How does this relate to the concept of *soul loss*? What ideas within our culture prevent us from living full and embodied lives? What does this have to do with trauma and shame?

THE THIRD GATE: THE SORROWS OF THE WORLD

The third gate opens to the sorrows of the world. And the world has a lot to grieve. Whether or not we consciously acknowledge it, the immense losses of habitat destruction, species extinction, and threatened earth-based lifeways imprint on our souls. While this grief is communal—and so much bigger than our human selves—we too often bear the pain of these losses alone, or fail to recognize them as losses at all.

1. Weller notes that this gate is where we most directly experience the "soul of the world," the *anima mundi*. What sights, feelings, sounds, or smells are evoked when you think of the soul of the world?

2. The soul of the world is known to peoples of every Indigenous culture. How do Indigenous communities where you live conceive of this relationship to the earth? If you're a settler whose ancestors aren't Indigenous to

the lands you live on, or if you don't know, try researching and see what you find.

Consider your ancestors. What place-based knowledge did they have? If you don't know, try researching and see what you find, or imagine how they may have connected to the soul of the world.

3. Weller says, "The cumulative grief of the world is overwhelming. The litany of losses could fill this book. . . . It takes a heart of courage and conviction, one willing to look into the center of the suffering and remain present."

   How do you think we can remain present to the grief of our planet?

   Do you think this is a useful or worthwhile endeavor? Why or why not?

4. Why do you think it's important to hold some of this grief instead of denying it or shutting it out?

5. How do you think moving through this kind of grief can help us become better activists, land defenders, earth stewards, or neighbors to the more-than-human world?

6. Have you ever felt the *anima mundi*? If yes, what was it like? What sights, sounds, or other sensations came up for you during this experience? If you haven't connected with the living earth in this way, would you like to?

7. Have you ever grieved for the losses of our planet? What was it like? Was there a single precipitating event, or have you felt into this grief more often?

   Did you recognize those feelings as grief at the time?

   Did you grieve alone, with other people, or with nature itself?

8. What kinds of community support or relationships might hold you as you feel into the suffering related to environmental destruction?

   How can you resource yourself and your community to move through grief together?

   What are your hopes and fears for the planet? What are your hopes, fears, and goals for this work?

9. Why do you think humans act as if we're separate from nature? What aspects of our culture promote this kind of thinking?

Do you feel *separate from* or a *part of* the earth? When? In what ways? Do you feel differently depending upon your location, company, or state of mind?

10. When you can, come to a quiet and comfortable place. With gentleness, think about an earth-based loss that brings you sorrow. What kind of ritual or practice could help you grieve this pain? How could you honor what's been lost?

     Who, if anyone, do you want to be there with you? How can this process help you care for what remains?

THE FOURTH GATE: WHAT WE EXPECTED AND DID NOT RECEIVE

There is another gate to grief. It can be difficult to identify, yet it's very present in each of our lives. This threshold into sorrow calls forth the things that we may not even realize we've lost: the connections, rites, and communities that nourish our souls—and are ours as a birthright.

1. Weller writes, "We are born expecting a rich and sensuous relationship with the earth and communal rituals of celebration, grief, and healing that keep us in connection with the sacred. . . . The absence of these requirements haunts us, even if we can't give them a name, and we feel their loss as an ache, a vague sadness that settles over us like a fog."

   Reflect on this quote. What do you think he means? Does it feel true to you? Does it speak to a longing you have, even if you've never expressed it consciously?

2. How do you think the container of a community, or your "village," can help us process grief?

3. What might be unlocked for you when you share grief with others instead of holding it on your own?

4. What might be different about our culture if we were all encouraged to share our grief together?

5. Do you want to share your grief journey with others? Why or why not?

6. Why do you think feelings like shame prevent us from allowing others to see our grief? Is there a relationship among shame, grief, and belonging?

7. Do you think that modern Western culture encourages us to isolate ourselves from our communities? What does this have to do with being "busy"?

8. Weller writes, "Facing our emptiness is key to our freedom . . . [but] it is important to remember that this emptiness is *not a reflection of personal failing, but a symptom of a wider loss.*" What do you think he means?

9. What do you think this emptiness has to do with modern Western culture's loss of connection to ancestral ways of knowing?

10. How do you think we could repair this connection? How could you begin to nurture this connection with your own circle or community?

THE FIFTH GATE: ANCESTRAL GRIEF

The fifth gate of grief is what Weller calls "ancestral grief." This is the grief we carry in our bodies from sorrows and pain experienced by those who came before us.

As you move through this work, you can think of your ancestors as your literal forebears. You can also consider those people whose legacies have shaped your shared experiences. Ancestors could be: queer ancestors, spiritual ancestors, community ancestors, cultural ancestors, or ancestors from your other lineages.

1. Many of our ancestors arrived in what is now called the United States after leaving their families, homes, and traditional lifeways behind. Some of our ancestors migrated voluntarily, others under duress, and others by force and enslavement. What are some of the stories of your ancestors? If you don't know for sure, that's okay. What do you think or imagine their stories might have been?

2. Weller writes, "These generations often survived without a feeling of home, living with only marginal connections with the Old Ways to guide them. The traditions that had nourished and held their people for hundreds, if not thousands, of years were difficult to sustain on the new continent. They lived betwixt and between the Old and the New Worlds, attempting to create something that would enable them to endure."

   How could this need to *endure* or *survive* have disrupted your ancestors' connection to their culture(s)?

3. Do you feel this loss too? If so, how?

4. Do you think that we each hold ancestral grief in our beings? Why or why not?

5. When you have some time, find a quiet and comfortable place to reflect. If it feels okay to do so, close your eyes. Think about your ancestors. What cultural knowing might have been lost or forcibly severed? What do you think it might have been like for them?

   What do you think it may have felt like in their bodies?

   What does it feel like in your body now, thinking of them?

6. Have you ever grieved for the losses of your ancestors? If so, what was it like?

   If not, do you think you might want or need to do so?

7. Weller shares the story of a woman he worked with. Her ancestral grief manifested in her body image, self-worth, and relationships. Does the lens of her story change how you see any of your own experiences? If so, how?

8. Some of our ancestors were the victims or survivors of oppression, enslavement, and genocide. Some of our ancestors were the perpetrators. Some of our bodies and family lines hold the echoes and actions of both. If any of these statements reflect the experiences or actions of your ancestors, how do you think that shows up in your own personal history or being as grief, if at all?

9. Weller shares that another facet of this grief is the loss *of* the ancestors. Many of us no longer look to our ancestral traditions as sources of connection with the powers of the world. This could be because those connections were severed; it may also be because we wish to distance ourselves from the harm that our ancestors perpetrated during their lifetimes, especially when those legacies of harm are braided into our social fabric today.

   Do you practice any kind of connection to your ancestors? Do you know what their traditions were, or what they might have been? If not, are you interested in nurturing a relationship with them?

   What comes up for you as you consider this work?

10. How might holding—and healing—our ancestral grief help us to move through the world differently?

    How could it impact our relationships with ourselves?

    With our communities?

    With the rest of the natural world?

Chapter 4

STORIES OF SORROW: RITUALS OF RENEWAL

*"Ritual is a means of attuning ourselves with one another,
to the land, and to the invisible worlds of spirit."*

Chapter 4: Questions for Reflection

1. This chapter opens with descriptions of two different healing rituals. Reflect on both. Does either resonate with you? Why or why not?

2. What is *ritual*? What kind of day-to-day rituals do you participate in? What meaning do they bring to your life, your relationships, or your connections with the world?

3. Weller notes, "Nearly every Indigenous culture has utilized ritual as a means of maintaining the health of the community. . . . Recovering this fundamental skill would help us better tend the needs of our soul and culture." What do you think he means?

4. Both rituals that Weller describes in the first two pages of this chapter embody something essential; neither practice is arbitrary. Each is rooted in the cosmology, culture, and lifeways of its people. Do you think that modern Western culture is fertile ground for such rituals? Why or why not?

5. Does your culture or cosmology support practices of connection and ritual? If so, how? If not, why do you think that might be?

6. Why do you think ritual helps us understand and move through grief and loss? How might a step-by-step process help us find meaning or integrate our experiences?

7. What do you think the relationship is between ritual and a safe, sacred space?

   What does "sacred space" mean to you?

8. Have you ever created or participated in a formal or informal ritual? This can be related to healing, but it doesn't have to be; it can also be a simple practice that you carry out in your daily life. Why do you do this ritual? When do you perform it? What function does it serve for you?

   If this ritual feels sacred or meaningful, were you conscious that you were being called to participate in a sacred act? How did this feel?

   When participating in ritual, do you experience your senses of time, connection, and physical sensation in the same or different ways as your "normal" life? If not in the same ways, what changes?

9. If you haven't participated in a grief or healing ritual, what do you think might be present for you? Are there pieces of yourself that you're hoping to tend or more deeply understand?

10. Which of your own sorrows calls on you to perform a healing ritual?

    What do you think you might want your ritual to look like?

    Where, and under what conditions, would it take place?

    Who else would you invite to participate? Consider the following practice to help guide you.

An Invitation Envisioning Ritual Practice

Choosing—or designing—a ritual that feels meaningful, honors your grief, and opens you to the transformative work ahead is a deeply personal endeavor. It can also feel like a daunting one. If you're ready to hold ritual space to begin metabolizing or relating differently to your grief, reflect upon the following. Consider, with gentleness and curiosity, what kind of container or practice could help you meet your grief with welcome, care, and presence.

1. WHAT YOU BRING; WHERE YOU'RE COMING FROM

When you have time and access to a quiet, peaceful place, think about your grief. What are you processing? What does this specific grief need from you in this moment? What might it ask of you over time? If you don't know, that's okay. What do you hope you might learn if you can open more fully to it?

Sit with this for as long as you'd like. What sights, sounds, sensations, or feelings come up? Allow these experiences to guide you as you consider the following: What are you bringing to the table? What is your grief bringing? What patterns, histories, narratives, or experiences are you coming from? Pay attention to what comes to the fore: If you're suffering the grief of environmental loss, for example, you may find that images of fire, water, plants, or a specific nature presence make themselves known. If you're grieving the loss of a beloved, you may find that specific memories or feelings come to your threshold. Look more deeply into what's resonating with you as you notice and explore. Allow your impressions and intuitions to act as a guide.

2. UNDERSTANDING INTENTION

Reflect on what you hope to gain from this ritual—and what your grief may need from it. How you show up to your practice shapes the texture and depth of your engagement. It can also help you make sense of what emerges.

Are you undertaking this practice to attune to your grief more fully, or to welcome in a new relationship with grief? To bear witness or hold space for what's been lost? Is your intention to build community with others, to come together in soulful presence? To create something beautiful and rich with meaning from your place of loss? Knowing what you wish to gain from your ritual—and being present to what your grief may ask of you in this moment—can bring insights into what might be right for the practice.

3. WHO—AND WHAT—WILL ACCOMPANY YOU?

Consider the following: Who will join you in your ritual? What qualities, energies, or skills feel important to ground in your practice?

Are there other beings—elements of the natural world, spirits, ancestors, guides, or other beloved presences—that you want to invoke or invite in?

What objects, symbols, offerings, or creations should be included? Think back to what came to the fore as you sat quietly with your grief. If you're having trouble or encountering resistance, consider turning to the natural world or a sacred setting to ask for inspiration. It's okay if you need to take extra time or come back to this practice later.

Where will the ritual take place? What practical considerations might shape the space in which you hold your ritual? If you're constrained by a location that may not be ideal, what could you bring in to alchemize your setting into holy ground? If you have access to nature, what elements call most strongly to you? Turn toward your grief as you feel into what needs tending, and consider what physical place feels nourishing to you, receptive to your grief, and respectful to approach.

4. CONSIDER THE PRACTICAL

Even when holding sacred space, practical matters come up. Here are some questions to get you thinking about ways to equip your container.

If your ritual includes symbolic action—like pouring water or burning an offering—what vessels will you use? If it will incorporate sound or music, what precautions need to be considered to respect others who share your space? If your ritual will last throughout the night, what can you bring to nourish your body, energize your spirit, and sustain the work? How will you honor the place—and the people of the place—in your ritual? How can you acknowledge or invite in the more-than-human beings who are present? How will you open the ritual space in a way that welcomes and anchors your work? How will you close it with reverence and gratitude?

5. DEEPENING YOUR EXPERIENCE

When your ritual closes, the work itself does not end. Return to your intention. What did your grief ask of you? What did the more-than-human world require of you? How can you continue to honor your grief—and embody an emerging and developing relationship with it—over the coming days, months, and years? This could be a daily practice like journaling, meditation, gratitude, art, communing with a person who's passed, or listening to spirit. It could also be a commitment to activism, community care, or a deepened relationship with other people or the earth. What feels right in your immediate period of integration? What feels realistic and doable today and beyond?

Chapter 5

SILENCE AND SOLITUDE: THE HOUSE OF OUR ALONENESS

The first half of *The Wild Edge of Sorrow* emphasizes the essential healing work that we can do in community and with the support of others. This next section moves into a more solitary space: the work we each must do on our own in the long breath of grief.

> *"Few of us live within community settings where we have continual access to touch and support. We will, in truth, spend many of our hours alone with our grief. In the cover of our solitude, we encounter another layer in our apprenticeship with sorrow. Here we are asked to hold an extended vigil with loss in the well of silence, slowly ripening our sorrow into something dense and gifting to the world."*

Chapter 5: Questions for Reflection

1. Silence and solitude are unavoidable facets of everyone's grief journeys. How do you think they each relate to healing?

2. Silence and solitude form an invitation to slow down, pause, and reflect. In what ways is this quiet contemplation at odds with modern Western culture?

3. Why might we each need to carve out spaciousness for silence and solitude in times of sorrow, bereavement, or healing?

4. When was the last time you truly slowed down and looked inward—whether you were grieving or not? What did you find? Did it feel comfortable? Uncomfortable? Surprising? Something else?

    If you don't know or can't recall, that's okay. What emotions, thoughts, images, or sensations come to mind as you think about slowing down? How does it feel in your body?

5. Weller notes that many of us have had experiences when our expressions of suffering were silenced: "Get over it." "Stop being so sensitive." "Other people have it worse." "You're wrong about what happened." Have you experienced this kind of silencing or shaming? By whom? What did it feel like emotionally? What did it feel like in your body?

6. Are you open to the idea that these experiences are wounds that need tending?

7. How can childhood wounds express themselves in grief, even decades later? What might these wounds look like? Below are some common examples of how people might express (or try to suppress) these wounds:
    - "I feel angry, but I don't know why."
    - "I dissociate with distractions."
    - "I numb myself with substances."
    - "I isolate myself from other people."
    - "I put all my energy into my work."
    - "My temper is explosive."
    - "I people-please."
    - "I do not allow myself to be vulnerable with others."

8. At times in our lives, we actively choose silence and solitude. Other times, as in the loss of a loved one, it's unwillingly forced upon us. Reflect on this

quote, chosen by Weller, from Rainer Maria Rilke: "I am too alone in the world, and not alone enough to make every minute holy."

What do you think Rilke means?

Why do you think Weller chose this quote?

What's coming up for you as you reflect on it?

What do you think these words might be trying to show us on our apprenticeship with sorrow?

9. How can silence and solitude help us turn toward our sorrows to do "the work in the deep"? Why is it important to turn toward our sorrows?

10. What do you think Weller means when he says, "Grief leads us back to the body through its wild, turning, heavy, twisting presence. And through the body, we are brought back again into the greater conversation with the living world"?

Writing Practice Freedom and Choice: Working with the Complex[*]

One of the primary tools that Weller has used in his own life and with countless others in gaining some separation from the complex has been a very specific writing process. The intention of the practice is to uncover the underlying premises and strategies that are developed inside the energetic field of the complex. We do this by writing out the "Worldview of the Child." Be mindful here, that when Weller uses the term *child*, he is not referring to the historical child we remember being. He uses the term to convey a style of perception that is undeveloped and primitive in its character.

We want to discern whose voice is speaking, whose story is being expressed in any given moment. Recall that the complex forms around a highly charged emotional situation, splitting off from consciousness and forming its own microcosm of existence. This partial self remains outside of consciousness until it is activated by a triggering event in our environment. At that point, we are often overtaken by the complex and become possessed by this other region of psyche. It is in this

---

[*] This is an adaptation of the "Freedom of Choice: Working with the Complex" ritual that appears in the resources section at the end of *The Wild Edge of Sorrow*.

state that we are locked within the cosmology of the complex, and the wider horizon of the adult presence is lost.

Complexes can form at any time in our life. What precipitates out of the traumatic experience is something primitive and undeveloped, which is why Weller uses the imagery of the child. When he speaks of the need to separate, he is saying that what we are separating from is the complex, not the child we once were. The child Weller is referring to in relation to the complex is a swirling wash of images, memories, perceptions, thoughts, and sensations that brings us into a style of being that is carried within the complex. The felt sense of this imaginal experience is akin to that of a child barely able to hold ground in the world—anxious and uncertain of its place and belonging. In the language of trauma, we are reduced to fight, flight, or freeze. We are brought to our most basic levels of survival.

The attitude we are seeking in the work of separation is one of affection and caring. It is akin to that of a parent responding to their child's distress. If we become too entangled in the pain, we are no longer able to be of help and comfort. The right distance in that moment is one of compassionate separation—witnessing, engaged, but separate.

Often, we can tell the complex has been present only after it has dissipated. The work of separating is intended to give us a way to stay present, especially when we are in triggering situations. The list Weller uses regarding the Worldview of the Child is intended to help us retain even the barest connection to the adult. The complex is a consolidation of perceptions that reflect a narrower band of possibility and imagination, so that when it is activated, our range of response becomes increasingly diminished. If we can remain rooted in the adult, we have a greater opportunity to live a life of choice rather than compulsion.

Write out the following in third person (he, she, their), the Worldview of the Child.

1. What are the child's basic assumptions?

   - About love

   - About power

   - About men

   - About women

   - About themselves

2. Based on these assumptions, what are the child's expectations in these same areas? For example: If the child holds an assumption that they are powerless, they would expect that they will always be one-down in relationships.

3. What strategies has the child employed to cope with the world that they are living in? For example: perfectionism, pleasing others, withdrawal, keeping everyone at a distance, self-preservation.

4. What triggers the child? What conditions bring the child to the foreground? For example: criticism, feeling abandoned, someone being angry, and so on.

5. How does the child show up in your experience?

   - Physically: What sensations do you notice when the complex arises? For example: tightness, heaviness, queasiness, shortness of breath, or shoulders rising.

   - Emotionally: What emotions do you notice when the complex is activated? For example: fear, shame, anxiety, or terror.

   - Mentally: What thoughts are you aware of when the complex is present? For example: mistrust or expectations of rejection or criticism.

6. What is the child protecting? One of Carl Jung's discoveries was that at the heart of every complex is a jewel of great price. When the complex was formed and splintered off from consciousness, it took a piece of something precious along with it to keep it safe. When one of Weller's complexes was resolved, spontaneity and joy returned to his life. It had not been safe to be spontaneous or joyful when he was fearful of being shamed for anything he did that might be seen as inappropriate. For Weller, it was wonderful to have his joy and spontaneity available once again.

This writing practice is meant to help us establish a beachhead, some little spot of turf that we can hold onto in hopes of keeping a connection with the adult. What we seek is the ability to encounter life openly, freely, and with soul. We cannot control what comes to us, what moods arise, what circumstances befall us. What we *can* do is work to maintain our adult presence, keeping it anchored and firmly rooted. This enables us to meet our life with compassion and to receive our suffering without judgments. This is a core piece in our apprenticeship with sorrow.

Chapter 6

PUSHING THROUGH SOLID ROCK

"Our culture, which wants to keep us busy and distracted twenty-four hours a day, keeps shunting grief to the background. We stand in the brightly lit areas of what is familiar and comfortable, not realizing we have lost something essential to the life of the soul."

Chapter 6: Questions for Reflection

1. Weller notes that many of us face challenges when we try to approach our grief—perhaps most notably that many of us live in a "flatline" culture, or a culture that avoids feeling into the depths. What do you think happens to our feelings when they become congested, both as individuals and on a collective scale?

2. Why do you think Weller chose to call this chapter "Pushing through Solid Rock"?

3. What is the notion of "private pain"? How do you see it showing up in our culture?

4. How has it shown up in your own life, family, or relationships?

5. Weller writes, "Facing the sorrows of the world requires that we remain intimate with the world." What do you think he means?

6. How does flatline culture push us away from becoming "intimate with the world"?

7. What implications do you think this has for our relationships? Our communities? Our ability to grieve?

8. What does it mean to "give our emotions a bottom"? How does this help us build trust in our ability to move through our pain?

9. How can communal rituals for grief and healing help us nurture a deeper relationship with our emotions? Why should we want that? What might prevent us from building this relationship?

10. How can tapping into our ability to grieve help us access—and embody— the full range of human joy and love?

An Invitation to Practice
Giving Emotions a Bottom Meditation

"If I go there, I'll never return." Weller writes of the fear and trepidation that many of us hold when we consider the immensity of feeling into or embodying our grief. For some of us, this may be the first time we've truly engaged with grief or welcomed its presence into our lives. It may be the first time we've offered it acknowledgment.

These fears are understandable: Modern Western culture doesn't teach us to put our faith in grief. Nor does it offer practices to explore the mysterious, sensuous, and multifaceted depths of our embodied emotionality. This short meditation invites you to recognize and feel into the fears that may prevent you from attuning to your grief.

THE PRACTICE

When you're able, find a still and quiet place and come to a comfortable position.

If it feels safe to do so, close your eyes or soften your gaze. Feel the ground beneath you. Bring attention to your breath, inhaling deeply and drawing out your exhale.

Bring attention to a feeling of pain, grief, loss, or discomfort. Welcome it in; in your mind's eye, set a place for it at your table. Notice what comes up for you as you consider this moment, this gesture: Do you feel open? Excited? Resistant? Scared?

Breathe into this feeling, especially if you feel fearful, hesitant, or closed off. If you notice that your attention is shifting or that your focus is slipping, gently call it back without judgment.

Notice what comes up for you in your body. Notice what comes up for you in your mind: an image, a vision, a memory, or a feeling. Bring your awareness here. Try to sit with it, even if you feel uncomfortable or scared. If it becomes too overwhelming, it's always okay to take a break and return to this exercise later.

Continue to breathe. On your inhale, acknowledge the feeling. On your exhale, ask what it's trying to convey.

Often our resistance to painful emotions betrays a lack of trust in our ability to hold them. We may fear becoming overwhelmed or falling apart. We may fear losing the illusion of control, or we may worry that we will fall apart. As you hold your grief or pain in this practice, consider where your resistance may originate. Explore this with your breath: Open to your grief on each inhale ("I meet you," "I accept you," "You are welcome," or "I see you"); acknowledge its potential message or teaching on each exhale. When you're ready to close this practice, offer yourself trust: You have the innate and immense capacity to hold difficult feelings, to move through them with skill and breath.

As Weller notes, *vesseling* is an essential component of grief work. It's also an act of maturity and care: When we engage difficult emotions—when we approach the depths with reverence and work them with intentionality—we honor the reality of our pain without displacing it onto others or the more-than-human world. We also find that we emerge. Getting to the bottom of our emotions is an important step in fortifying the containers that can alchemize our pain. Listening to our feelings—and accepting that we have difficult feelings—is a vital starting point.

Chapter 7

DRINKING THE TEARS OF THE WORLD

"Coming home to grief is sacred work, a powerful practice that confirms what the Indigenous soul knows and what spiritual traditions teach: We are connected to one another. Our fates are bound together in a mysterious but recognizable way."

Chapter 7: Questions for Reflection

1. Why do you think Weller says, "Grief work [is] a core element in our ability to sustain and maintain the well-being of our communities"?

    Do you think that grief can be an *act of responsibility* to the world? Why or why not?

2. Do you think that grief work could impact how loss is held in your own community? Why or why not?

3. Weller notes that grief work is also "a form of soul protest, our wholehearted response to acts of violence and oppression." What do you think he means? Can you think of any examples?

4. Many of us are impacted by systemic harms, from the destruction of our planet to identity-based injustice. What role do you think grief work can play in community organizing or justice movements? To what end?

5. "Grief is the work of mature people." Do you agree or disagree? Why?

   What other characteristics do you think people should strive to embody as they embark on grief and soul work?

6. Weller shares a Swedish fairy tale about the immense transformational power of being seen in our vulnerability—especially when that vulnerability has been hidden away. What came up for you as you read this story? Did you relate to any of the characters? If so, whom? Why?

7. Why do you think Weller chose to call this chapter "Drinking the Tears of the World"? What do you think it means to "drink the tears of the world"?

8. Many of us develop coping skills to get through the day. Some of us need them to help us navigate certain periods of our lives. Do you know what some of your coping mechanisms are? If you're having trouble recognizing one, consider some common examples:

   - "I drink coffee throughout the day."
   - "I clean my space."
   - "I work out for an hour after work."
   - "I smoke or drink."
   - "I listen to my favorite song on repeat."
   - "I pray or talk to Spirit."
   - "I numb myself out."
   - "I avoid being alone."

   When have those coping mechanisms helped you? What do you think about them? Here are some examples to get you thinking about it:

   - "Doing this thing protected me at a time when I couldn't fall apart."
   - "They helped me grieve incrementally; everything was so intense, and I couldn't process all of it at once."
   - "My coping mechanisms helped me go to work, complete my tasks, and engage with others."
   - "I was able to keep it together so I could be there for my kids, family, or friends."

Do you think coping mechanisms ever get in the way of feeling your grief? Of healing? Why or why not?

9. Sometimes the time comes to thank our coping skills for what they've offered us, then gently let them go. Do you have any coping mechanisms that don't serve you anymore?

    What might it mean to release them? To be *ready* to release them?

    What kind of ritual would you design to help you mark this part of your grief journey?

10. While many of us only think about grief in relation to the death of a loved one, we have a lot to grieve. A ritual that Weller describes in this chapter relates to illness, stress, and the weight of carrying grief without community.

    When you're grieving, what are some of your unique emotional needs?

    What would support look like to you? How do you think you can ask for it?

An Invitation to Ritual Speaking to the Earth*

"This ritual is common among many cultures, and we have adapted it for our use. This ritual is often experienced alone, though you can invite witnesses to join you. It is useful for those times when you are alone and feel the need to move grief out of your body. The deep truth that emerges from this ritual, however, is that you are never fully alone. In this particular ritual, you come to feel the loving pulse of the earth surrounding you.

"Find a place outdoors that feels utterly safe. It may be your backyard, a friend's backyard, or a place in the wild. Dig an opening in the earth big enough for you to speak into, approximately a foot wide and a foot deep. Begin by saying some words of gratitude to the earth for being able to receive your grief. Place some tobacco or ash—which are often used in traditional cultures as offerings—or any offering you feel is right for you into the hole as you say your words of gratitude. Then let the earth know what you need. You can say something like, 'I have been carrying this grief for so long, and I cannot hold it any longer. It is too big for me. It is weighing me down and depriving me of any joy. I know you can hold this sorrow. In fact, you can turn it into something sweet for the roots that rest in your

---

* The "Speaking to the Earth" ritual appears in the resources section at the end of *The Wild Edge of Sorrow*.

body. I do this to set down my sorrows so I can better participate in the mending of our community. Thank you for being here for me and all of us.'

"Then, lying on your belly, speak, weep, cry, or scream your grief into the earth. She is able to take it all in and will reshape it into nutrients for all life. When you are done, it is important for you to thank the earth for her loving and holding. Close the opening and leave it as close as possible to how you found it, so no one would know that something had happened in this spot."

Chapter 8

ENTERING THE HEALING GROUND: THE SACRED WORK OF GRIEF

"Whenever we touch the places of loss in our lives, at whatever gate they appear, we move closer to the earth. We become more intimate with our surroundings and lean in to those we love. At least, that is the invitation that true grieving offers to us."

Chapter 8: Questions for Reflection

1. Why do you think Weller chose to open this chapter with the William Blake quote "The deeper the sorrow, the greater the joy"?

2. As you've worked your way through *The Wild Edge of Sorrow* and this workbook, have your thoughts on the relationship between sorrow and joy changed? If yes, how? If not, why?

3. Weller describes grief as "Night Work" that "drop[s] us into a world the color of a raven's wings." How would you describe the work of grief? What images, sounds, feelings, or sensations come to you when you think about grief?

4. What do you think Weller means by "initiation"?

5. How does the idea of *initiation* relate to the power of ritual and the transformation of renewal?

   In what ways does grief function as an initiation?

6. The duality of lightness and darkness is present in many characterizations of how we experience grief, loss, death, rebirth, and renewal. What ideas does modern Western culture hold about darkness?

7. What do you think modern Western culture misses here?

8. What does it mean to "befriend the darkness" within the context of grief? As individuals, what might we gain from doing so?

9. What collective transformations or insights do you think we could have by befriending our grief?

10. Reflect on the quote: "Every loss, personal or shared, prepares us for our own time of leaving. Letting go is not a passive state of acceptance but a recognition of the brevity of all things. This realization invites us to love fully now, in this moment, when what we love is here."

    Why do you think Weller said this? What are your takeaways, if any?

11. What is the relationship between grief and gratitude?

    How can this bear on our ability to let go when the time comes?

    How can this reveal an invitation to love more fully, now and in this moment, "when what we love is here"?

Chapter 9

BECOMING ANCESTORS

*"[Sometimes] this consuming grief comes from outside
of our immediate world, gathering like storm
clouds in the distance and then, in a thunderous
clap, falling on us with a drenching rain."*

Chapter 9: Questions for Reflection

1. Weller acknowledges, "Sometimes it's all too much. Sometimes the cup of sorrows is not merely full, it's overflowing, and our capacity to stand upright is mightily challenged."

   Think about a time when this has been true for you. Weller chooses the metaphor of a cup. What imagery or idea best represents this all-too-much state for you?

2. In the opening of this chapter, Weller describes a time when the "bough broke" for him. He notes that the suicide of an acquaintance "released a cascade of feeling I was carrying for . . . our death-dealing, nature-consuming, hell-bent-on-our-collective-demise society. My interior denial systems were shattered, along with the fantasies of our somehow figuring our way through the eye of the needle in the nick of time. . . . Everything was clouded—shrouded actually—some veil coming between me and life."

   Have you ever experienced grief that opened you up to the sorrows of your community, the culture, or the world? If yes, what happened?

3. Weller offers several things that helped his heart "find bottom": picking up a book that spoke to what his soul needed. Organizing. Building bookshelves. Moving things around again, both literally and metaphorically.

   How do you move through your own periods of all-too-much grief? Are you moving through one now? What helps you "return to participating in the daily rhythms of life"?

4. What do you think these periods of grief tell you about yourself, if anything? Why?

5. What do you think these periods of grief reveal to you about our culture or the world, if anything? Why?

6. What does Weller mean by embodying "good manners" with the earth and future generations?

   Amid all we have to grieve, do you think *good manners* matter? Why or why not?

7. Weller returns to the question, "What good does it do to grieve?"

   What good *does* it do to grieve?

8. Do you think your thoughts on this question are different now than when you started this workbook? Why or why not? And if so, how?

9. At the end of this chapter's description of a drumming ritual, Weller states, "We were ancestors in training." What do you think it means to be an "ancestor in training"?

   What does this have to do with grief?

10. *The Wild Edge of Sorrow* closes, in part, with this thought: "So much in this world needs our attention. So much is threatened and clinging perilously to the edge of existence. We know this is true. Grief is our witness to these painful realities. Grief is also our response that confirms our intimate bond with all creation. When we leave here, it is essential that we feel that we did all we could for the generations to come, for this sweet earth, for all we loved."

    Reflect on the quote above. Do you agree or disagree? When you reflect on "all you love," what comes to the fore?

An Invitation to Ritual The Stone Ritual*

"In this ritual, a shrine is created that has a large bowl of water at its center. Surrounding this bowl is a collection of small stones, each small enough to fit easily in the palm of your hand. After an invocation is made, participants approach the shrine, one at a time, pick up a stone, and speak aloud, if they wish, a grief they are carrying in their hearts.

"When they have finished speaking that particular sorrow, they place the stone into the bowl of water. It could be sorrow over any particular loss, the suffering of their children, or the wild ravages that are happening to the earth and her creatures. Any and all grief is invited to the bowl. This is repeated until everyone has approached the shrine. A group can decide ahead of time whether people will be able to go to the shrine more than once. Usually, people can go as often as needed. As all the sorrows are named and the bowl fills, there is a growing sense that this is a *collective* grief, not just an individual's. It is ours.

"After a short pause to let this truth sink into our bones, someone picks up the bowl, and there is a procession outside, where the water is poured onto a plant, taking our grief and turning it into nourishment for the green world. Someone then agrees to take the stones to a river, a pond, or the ocean, so the movements of the water can scour these stones clean once again. This is a simple yet powerful ritual.

"This ritual has been used in many settings: a community dealing with the suicide of one of its youths; a group of activists protesting a logging action along the Canadian border; and as a process for a monthly grief circle."

---

* "The Stone Ritual" appears in the resources section at the end of *The Wild Edge of Sorrow*.

About the Authors

Francis Weller is a psychotherapist, writer, and soul activist. He is a master of synthesizing diverse streams of thought from psychology, anthropology, mythology, alchemy, Indigenous cultures, and poetic traditions. He has introduced the healing work of ritual to thousands of people. He founded and currently directs WisdomBridge, an organization that offers educational programs that seek to integrate the wisdom from Indigenous cultures with the insights and knowledge gathered from Western poetic, psychological, and spiritual traditions. His writings have appeared in anthologies and journals exploring the confluence between psyche, nature, and culture, including *The Sun* magazine, the *Utne Reader*, *Kosmos* Journal, and *Ruminate*. He is the author of *The Wild Edge of Sorrow* and is currently completing his fourth book, *Facing the World with Soul and Why It Matters*.

Bevin Donahue lives in New England. She works for North Atlantic Books.

About North Atlantic Books

North Atlantic Books (NAB) is an independent, nonprofit publisher committed to a bold exploration of the relationships between mind, body, spirit, and nature. Founded in 1974, NAB aims to nurture a holistic view of the arts, sciences, humanities, and healing. To make a donation or to learn more about our books, authors, events, and newsletter, please visit www .northatlanticbooks.com.